Get pupils' knowledge in order with CGP!

Looking for a simple way to help pupils learn all the key facts for Year 5 Science?
Well, look no further — this Knowledge Organiser is the perfect solution!

We've condensed each topic down to the key facts, so it covers
exactly what pupils need, with clear diagrams and tables.

And that's not all! There's a matching Year 5 Science Knowledge Retriever — a
great way of making sure pupils have got to grips with the facts on every page.

CGP – still the best! ☺

Our sole aim here at CGP is to produce the highest quality books —
carefully written, immaculately presented and dangerously close to being funny.

Then we work our socks off to get them out to you
— at the cheapest possible prices.

Published by CGP.

Editors: Josie Gilbert, Paul Jordin, Jake McGuffie, Luke Molloy, Rachael Rogers, Charlotte Sheridan and George Wright

Contributor: Paddy Gannon

With thanks to Glenn Rogers and Kate Whitelock for the proofreading.

With thanks to Jan Greenway for the copyright research.

ISBN: 978 1 78908 953 0

Printed by Elanders Ltd, Newcastle upon Tyne.

Clipart from Corel®

Illustrations by: Sandy Gardner Artist, email sandy@sandygardner.co.uk

Based on the classic CGP style created by Richard Parsons.

Contents

Reproduction

Reproduction

Reproduction: When new living things are made, e.g. baby animals or new plants.

Two types of reproduction:

1 Asexual
Only one parent needed.

2 Sexual
Two parents needed — a male and a female.

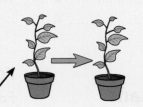

Animal Reproduc[tion]

Animals reproduce by sexual reproduction

Egg from female

Sperm from male

Plant Reproduction — Sexual

Stigma: Female part of flower.

Pollen: From male part of flower.

Pollination — pollen transferred to the stigma of another plant.

Egg fertilised by the pollen.

Fertilised egg becomes a seed.

Seed germinates into a seedling.

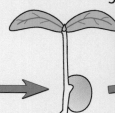

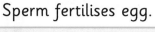
Sperm fertilises egg.

Fertilised egg becomes an embryo.

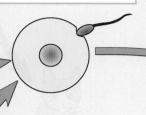

Sexual reproduction happens like this in other animals too, not just humans.

Embryo grows into a baby.

Seedling grows into a plant.

In asexual reproduction, new plants grow from parts of a parent plant (without using pollen and eggs).

Gardeners can use this method, e.g.:

1 Start with the parent plant.

2 Cut off small parts.

3 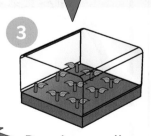 Put the small parts in soil.

4 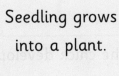 The small parts grow into new plants.

A plant growing from a bulb is also an example of asexual reproduction.

Life Cycles: Animals

Life Cycles

Life cycle — the series of changes a living thing goes through during its life, including reproduction.

The Cat Life Cycle

Cats are **mammals**.
Their life cycle starts with a fertilised egg growing inside the mother.

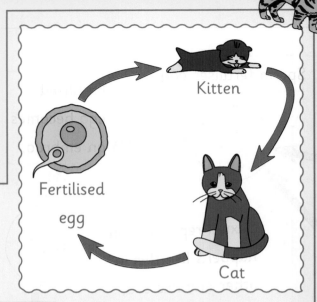

Fertilised egg

Kitten

Cat

The Owl Life Cycle

Owl

Eggs

Chick

Mammals, like humans, give birth to live babies.

Owls are **birds**.
Their life cycle starts with the mother laying fertilised eggs in a nest.

The chick develops inside the egg, and later hatches from the egg.

The Butterfly Life Cycle

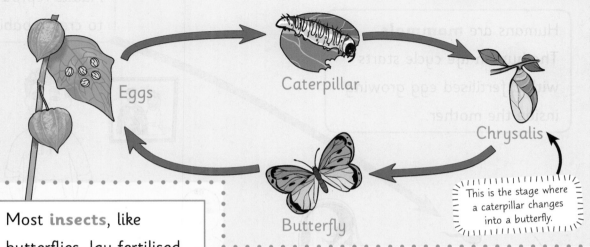

Eggs

Caterpillar

Chrysalis

Butterfly

This is the stage where a caterpillar changes into a butterfly.

Most **insects**, like butterflies, lay fertilised eggs near a food source. E.g. many butterflies lay eggs onto the leaves and branches of plants.

The Frog Life Cycle

Frogs are **amphibians**.
Their life cycle starts with the mother laying fertilised eggs in water.

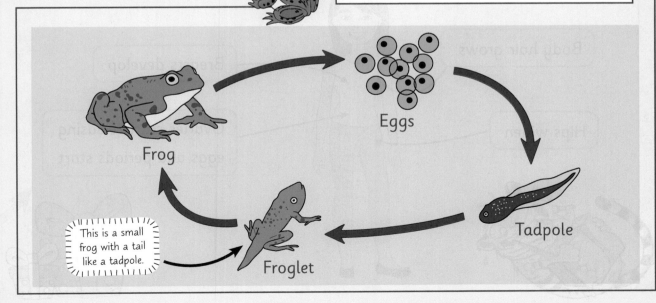

Frog

Eggs

Tadpole

Froglet

This is a small frog with a tail like a tadpole.

Life Cycles: Humans

Human Life Cycle

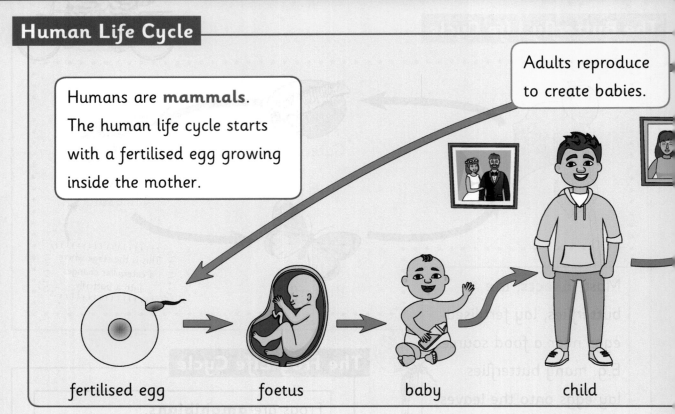

Humans are **mammals**. The human life cycle starts with a fertilised egg growing inside the mother.

Adults reproduce to create babies.

fertilised egg   foetus   baby   child

Puberty — Girls

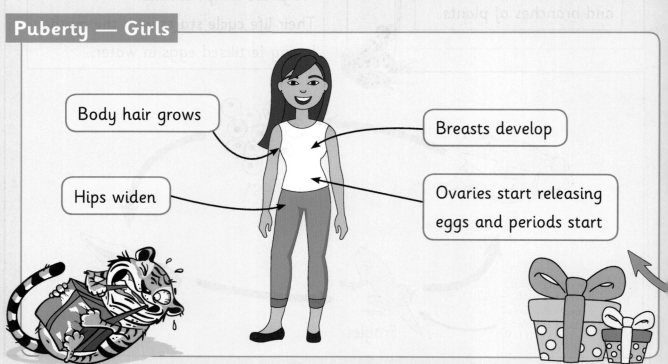

Body hair grows

Breasts develop

Hips widen

Ovaries start releasing eggs and periods start

adolescent   adult   old age   death

Puberty happens during **adolescence**.

Puberty

Puberty — body changing between 10 and 18 years.

Different for girls and boys.

Puberty — Boys

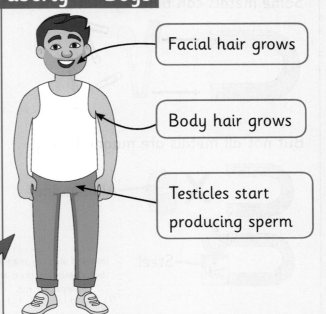

Facial hair grows

Body hair grows

Testicles start producing sperm

Comparing Everyday Materials

Hardness

Hard materials are difficult to scratch or bend. E.g.

steel hammer

diamond-edged saw

Materials that aren't hard are soft. E.g.

cushions and mattresses

Transparency

Transparent materials are see-through, e.g. glass.

Opaque materials are not see-through, e.g. thick curtain fabric.

Different materials have different properties, e.g. hard, soluble, magnetic, etc. The properties of a material affect what we use it for.

Magnetic Materials

Some metals can be magnetic (attracted to magnets), while non-metals can't.

But not all metals are magnetic, e.g.

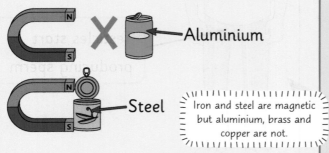

— Aluminium

— Steel

Iron and steel are magnetic but aluminium, brass and copper are not.

Conductors of Electricity

Electricity can flow through electrical conductors.

E.g. metal pins and copper wire.

Solubility

Insoluble materials don't dissolve, e.g. metal spoon and ceramic mug.

Soluble materials dissolve, e.g. sugar cubes.

Conductors of Heat

Thermal insulators don't let much heat pass through them. E.g the wooden spoon and the plastic handle.

Thermal conductors let heat pass through them easily. E.g. the metal pan.

Thermal insulators can keep heat in or out. E.g. warm clothes

drink flask for hot or cold drinks

Never touch bare or frayed wires — electricity can be conducted through wires into your body, giving you an electric shock.

Electrical insulators can't carry electricity. E.g. the plastic case and insulated flex are safe to touch without getting a shock.

Wood, plastic, glass and rubber are all electrical insulators. Most metals are good electrical conductors.

Separating & Changing Materials

Dissolving

Some solids dissolve in liquids to form a solution.

For example:

Sugar dissolves in tea and coffee.

Gravy granules dissolve in water.

> When a solid dissolves, you can't see it anymore.

Mixtures

Rice in water

A solution of salt and water

A mixture is just things mixed together.

Peas mixed with potatoes

Separating Mixtures

The separating method depends on the mixture:

If a solid is:

dissolved in a liquid

mixed with another solid

mixed with a liquid

1 Sieving — e.g. to separate peas from potatoes.

Use a mesh sieve.

The bigger bits don't go through.

The smaller bits do.

2 Filtering — e.g. to separate tea leaves from tea.

3 Evaporation — e.g. to separate sugar from a sugar solution.

Heat the solution.

The liquid evaporates.

The solid is left behind.

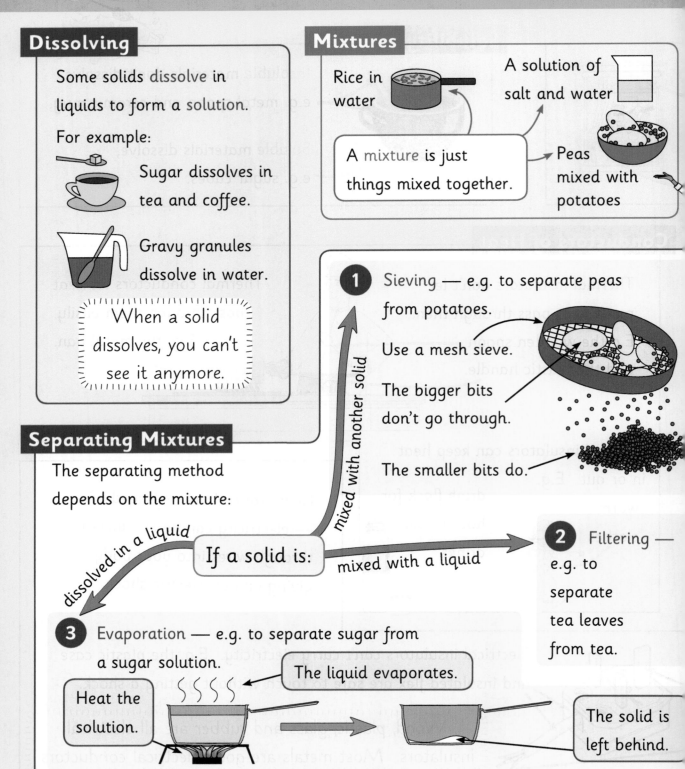

Reversible Changes

After a reversible change, the material looks and feels different, but it can change back to how it was before the change. Three examples:

1

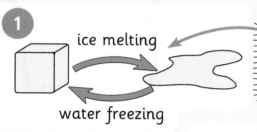

ice melting

water freezing

All changes of state are reversible.

2 mixing beans and rice

sieving

3

dissolving sugar in water

sugar solution

sugar

evaporating

---

1 Burning wood to form ash.

2 Baking a cake mixture into a cake.

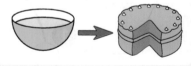

3 Reacting bicarbonate of soda with vinegar to produce carbon dioxide.

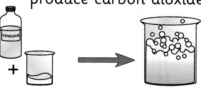

VINEGAR

+

Irreversible Changes

After an irreversible change, a completely different material is formed, and it can't change back to how it was before the change.

Three examples:

The filter stops the solid.

The liquid passes through.

The Planets, Earth, Sun and Moon

The Solar System

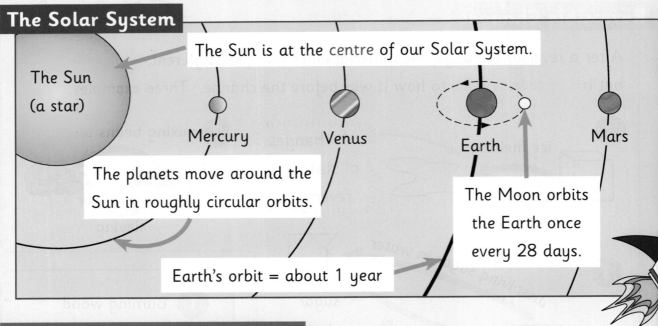

The Sun is at the centre of our Solar System.

The Sun (a star)

Mercury

Venus

Earth

Mars

The planets move around the Sun in roughly circular orbits.

The Moon orbits the Earth once every 28 days.

Earth's orbit = about 1 year

Viewing the Moon from Earth

We see the Moon because it reflects light from the Sun. The view of the Moon from Earth changes as it orbits. The view depends on how much light shines on the side we can see.

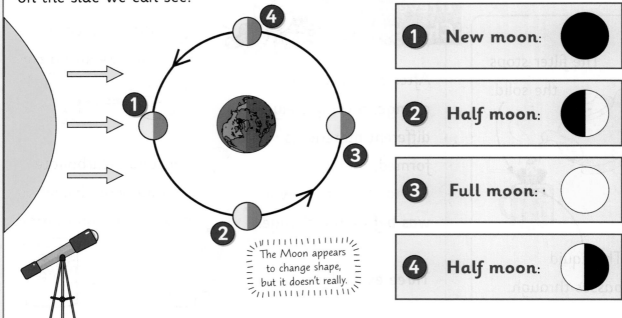

The Moon appears to change shape, but it doesn't really.

1 **New moon:**

2 **Half moon:**

3 **Full moon:**

4 **Half moon:**

Jupiter

Saturn

Uranus

Neptune

Earth isn't the only planet with a moon — some other planets, like Jupiter, have moons too.

All eight planets, the Sun and the Moon are roughly spherical (round).

Night and Day

Night and day are caused by the Earth rotating (spinning on its axis). 1 full rotation = 24 hours = 1 day.

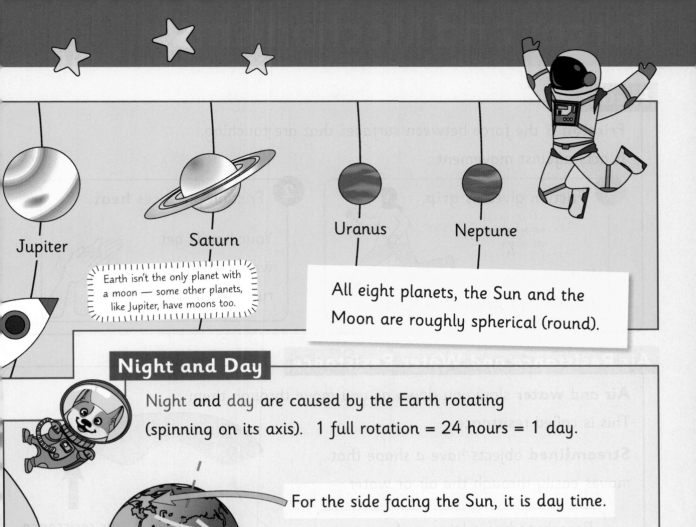

For the side facing the Sun, it is day time.

For the side facing away from the Sun, it is night time.

The Sun is a very strong light source — the light from it can damage your eyes. You should <u>never</u> look directly at the Sun, even if you're wearing sunglasses.

The Earth's rotation causes the Sun to appear to move across the sky:

Sunrise in the East

Sunset in the West

Forces and Mechanisms

Friction

Friction is the force between surfaces that are touching.

It acts against movement.

1 Friction gives us **grip**.

Trainer soles have lots of grip.

Without grip, starting and stopping is hard.

2 Friction produces **heat**.

Your hands get warm when you rub them together.

Air Resistance and Water Resistance

Air and **water** slow you down as you move through them. This is called resistance.

Streamlined objects have a shape that moves easily through the air or water.

Parachute has a large surface area so it moves slowly through the air.

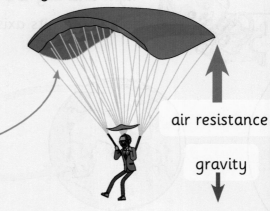

air resistance

gravity

driving force

Streamlined car moves quickly through the air.

air resistance

streamlined shark

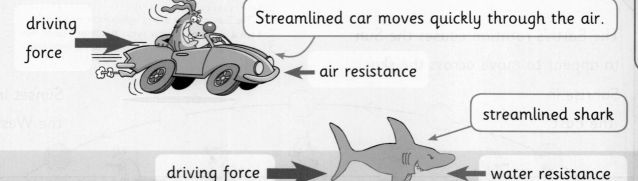

driving force

water resistance

Gravity

Gravity acts between objects and the Earth. It pulls objects towards the centre of the Earth.

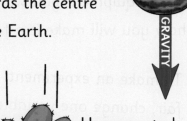

Unsupported objects fall towards the Earth.

Things on the ground are pulled down by gravity too.

That's why you can't fall off the Earth.

Levers, Pulleys and Gears

Levers

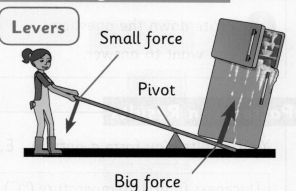

Small force

Pivot

Big force

Pulleys

Pulling down on the rope lifts the heavy object. It's easier than picking it up.

Gears

When you turn the big gear —

— the small gear will turn faster.

non-streamlined human

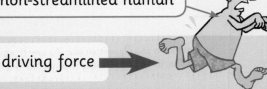

driving force

It's difficult to run in water because it pushes against you.

water resistance

Working Scientifically

Planning an Experiment

1 Write down the question you want to answer.

2 Write a method for the experiment. This should include:

- what you will measure/observe,
- what equipment you will use,
- how you will make it a fair test.

To make an experiment fair, change one variable at a time and keep everything else the same. (A variable is anything that could affect your results.)

Patterns in Results

Your results may form a pattern. E.g.:

Thickness (mm)	Temperature (°C)
4	54
8	58
12	62
16	41

Results that don't fit the pattern might suggest that a mistake has been made in your experiment.

If possible, repeat your experiment a few times to make sure your results are reliable.

Displaying Results

Think about how best to display your results.

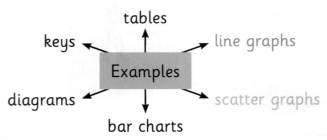

tables

keys → Examples ← line graphs

diagrams

bar charts

scatter graphs

The best way depends on your experiment.

Conclusions

Your experiment should end with a conclusion — a sentence that sums up your findings.

The sentence is usually written like: 'As one thing changes like this, another thing changes like this.'

3 Make a prediction
(what you think will happen).

Line Graphs

Plot your results on a grid,
then join them up with straight lines.

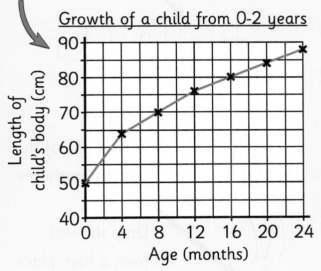

Growth of a child from 0-2 years

Line graphs are often used to show how something changes over time.

Scatter Graphs

Plot your results on a
grid, then draw one line that
goes as close to all the points
as possible.

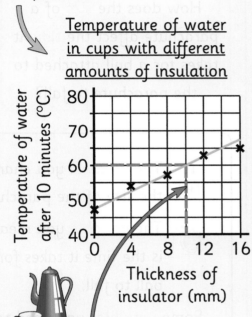

Temperature of water
in cups with different
amounts of insulation

By drawing from the x-axis to the line, then across to the y-axis, you can predict the temperature for different thicknesses, e.g.: 'The temperature will be 60 °C when the insulator is 10 mm thick.'

Explain whether there were any
problems with your experiment:

- Did you make any mistakes?
- Did all the results fit with the pattern?
- Could the test have been more fair?

Problems with the experiment might mean your results are not reliable — if so, you might want to do further tests.

Investigation – Falling Objects

Planning your Experiment

1 What question do you want to answer?

How does the size of a parachute affect the time it takes for a ball attached to the parachute to fall?

A
B The variable you change is the size of the parachute.

The variable you measure is the time it takes for the ball to fall.

Some variables you need to control (keep the same) are:

- the ball you use,
- where the ball is dropped from,
- the conditions (e.g. the wind).

2 How will you do your experiment?

1. Make five square parachutes out of paper, each one with a different side length. Use a ruler to measure the side lengths.

2. Attach one of the paper parachutes to a ball. Drop the ball from a high place (e.g. a balcony or window).

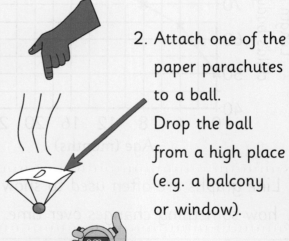

3. Using a stopwatch, get someone standing on the ground to measure the time between the ball being dropped and it reaching the ground.

4. Repeat steps 2 and 3 for all five parachutes.

3 What do you predict will happen?

↓

The larger the parachute, the longer it will take the ball to fall.

Side length of paper parachute (cm)	10	20	30	40	50
Time taken for the ball to fall to the ground (s)	2	4	6	7	9

It'd be good practice to repeat the experiment a few times to make sure these results are reliable.

You could plan similar experiments to test further questions, for example:

 How does the shape of the parachute affect the time it takes the ball to fall?

 How does the weight of the ball affect the time it takes to fall?

Time taken for a ball to fall with different parachutes attached

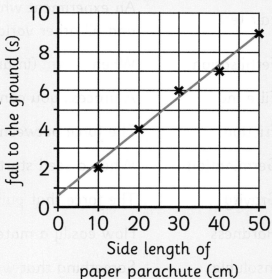

Y-axis: Time taken for ball to fall to the ground (s)

X-axis: Side length of paper parachute (cm)

You can make predictions based on your results that you could test with further experiments. E.g. you could use the graph to predict how long it would take a ball with no parachute attached to fall.

Conclusion

The results show that the larger the parachute is, the more time it takes for the ball to fall to the ground.

Glossary

Air resistance	Air pushing back against an object moving through it.
Asexual reproduction	In plants, when part of a parent plant grows into a new plant. Asexual reproduction requires only one parent.
Conclusion	A simple sentence that sums up what you found out in an experiment.
Conductor	A material that lets heat or electricity pass through it.
Dissolve	When a solid breaks up completely in a liquid to make a solution.
Evaporating	When a liquid is heated up and changes into a gas. It can be used to separate a solid from a liquid that it is dissolved in.
Fair test	An experiment where only one variable is changed, and all other variables are controlled (kept the same).
Fertilisation	When sperm (in animals) or pollen (in plants) joins with an egg.
Filtering	A process you can use to separate a solid from a liquid.
Friction	The force between touching surfaces that acts against movement.
Germination	When a seed starts to sprout and grow into a seedling.
Gravity	The force that pulls everything towards the centre of the Earth.
Hardness	How easily a material can be scratched or bent.
Insoluble	Something that won't dissolve in a liquid.
Insulator	A material that won't let heat or electricity pass through it.
Irreversible change	A change where you can't get the starting materials back once the change has happened.
Life cycle	The stages that a plant or animal goes through during its life.
Magnetic	A material that's attracted to a magnet.
Mixture	When two or more different materials are mixed together.

Moon	A large, natural object that orbits a planet. Different planets have different numbers of moons.
Opaque	A material that you can't see through.
Orbit	The path an object takes around another object in space.
Pollination	When pollen is carried from one flower to the stigma of another.
Prediction	What you think will happen in an experiment.
Puberty	When the body changes and develops during adolescence.
Reproduction	Making new living things — animals have babies, plants grow new plants.
Reversible change	A change that can be undone — you can get the starting materials back once the change has happened.
Sexual reproduction	When an egg is fertilised and then grows into a new plant or animal.
Sieving	Using a mesh to separate larger solid objects from smaller ones.
Solar system	The Sun and the things that orbit it, including Earth and the other planets.
Soluble	Something that will dissolve in a liquid.
Solution	A mixture formed when a solid dissolves in a liquid.
Streamlined	When an object has a smooth shape so that movement through air or water is easier.
Sun	The star in the centre of our solar system.
Transparent	A material that you can see through.
Variable	A factor in an experiment that you can control, change or measure.
Water resistance	Water pushing back against an object moving through it.

Index